D0712945

TEAM EARTH

POLLINATORS
ANIMALS HELPING PLANTS THRIVE

BY MARTHA LONDON

CONTENT CONSULTANT
Etya Amsalem, PhD
Assistant Professor of Entomology
Pennsylvania State University

Core Library
An Imprint of Abdo Publishing
abdobooks.com

Cover image: Bees help pollinate many kinds
of flowers.

abdobooks.com

Published by Abdo Publishing, a division of ABDO, PO Box 398166, Minneapolis, Minnesota 55439. Copyright © 2020 by Abdo Consulting Group, Inc. International copyrights reserved in all countries. No part of this book may be reproduced in any form without written permission from the publisher. Core Library™ is a trademark and logo of Abdo Publishing.

Printed in the United States of America, North Mankato, Minnesota
092019
012020

THIS BOOK CONTAINS
RECYCLED MATERIALS

Cover Photo: Dirk Daniel Mann/Shutterstock Images
Interior Photos: Dirk Daniel Mann/Shutterstock Images, 1; Jennifer Bosvert/Shutterstock Images, 4–5; Randee Daddona/Shutterstock Images, 6; Blue Ring Media/Shutterstock Images, 9; Yunhyok Choi/Shutterstock Images, 12–13; Paul Reeves Photography/Shutterstock Images, 15, 43; Jean Landry/iStockphoto, 18; Dan Wrench/iStockphoto, 20; Harry Collins/iStockphoto, 22–23; Wim Hoek/iStockphoto, 25, 45; Marvin Minder/Shutterstock Images, 27; Rolf Nussbaumer/ImageBroker/Newscom, 28; Ian Grainger/Shutterstock Images, 30–31; Jeffrey B. Banke/Shutterstock Images, 33; Red Line Editorial, 35; April Bartholomew/The Morning Call/AP Images, 39

Editor: Marie Pearson
Series Designer: Megan Ellis

Library of Congress Control Number: 2019942119

Publisher's Cataloging-in-Publication Data

Names: London, Martha, author.
Title: Pollinators: animals helping plants thrive / by Martha London
Other Title: animals helping plants thrive
Description: Minneapolis, Minnesota : Abdo Publishing, 2020 | Series: Team earth | Includes online resources and index.
Identifiers: ISBN 9781532191008 (lib. bdg.) | ISBN 9781644943274 (pbk.) | ISBN 9781532176852 (ebook)
Subjects: LCSH: Pollinators--Juvenile literature. | Pollination by insects--Juvenile literature. | Pollination by animals--Juvenile literature. | Plant ecology--Juvenile literature. | Plants--Reproduction--Juvenile literature.
Classification: DDC 571.8642--dc23

CONTENTS

PLANTS NEED POLLINATORS

The blue orchard bee crawls out of her reed tube. She doesn't live in a hive with other bees. But her tube is near other orchard bees. She is a type of mason bee.

As the bee leaves her home, she looks for pollen and nectar. The spring air is cool. The sky is overcast. Clouds block out most of the sunlight.

The bee's body is dark blue. Her wings buzz as she makes her way to an apple blossom. At the center of the white flower are orange stamens. Stamens look like tall

Blue orchard bees pollinate orchards, including those with plum trees.

stems in the blossom. Stamens are organs that produce pollen. A stamen is made up of two parts. The filament is the stem-like portion. The anther is the bud-like top. Pollen collects on the anthers. When the bee lands on the flower, some of the pollen dusts off onto her body. Nectar sits at the bottom of the blossom. The bee eats the nectar. Nectar is high in sugar. She also eats some of the pollen. It is a good source of protein. She collects some to bring to her young too. When she's finished with the flower, she flies off.

SOCIAL OR NOT?

Honeybees are very social. They are protective of their nests. Mason bees and ground-nesting bees are different. They live alone. They are not as protective of their nests. Most bees native to North America are solitary. They are unlikely to sting. Blue orchard bees are especially calm. They are great bees to keep. They pollinate in early spring. It takes just ten bees to pollinate an entire tree of flowers.

Some farmers keep blue orchard bees to pollinate their orchards. Each bee nests in its own hollow tube.

As she lands on a bloom in another tree, the pollen from the previous flower falls off. This pollinates the flower she landed on. Soon an apple will begin to form.

Blue orchard bees are very efficient. It takes just 300 bees to pollinate 1 acre (0.4 ha) of apple trees. Apple blossoms don't bloom long. There is just a short time for pollination. Thanks to blue orchard bees, each acre of apple trees can produce up to 30,000 apples.

A HUGE SYSTEM

A few species of trees and plants use wind pollination. This is the process of pollen blowing from one flower to another in the wind. However, as much as 95 percent of the world's plants rely on pollinators. Studies estimate that 300,000 species of plants use animal pollinators. Of those pollinators, most are insects. There are 16,000 bee species. Approximately 1,000 vertebrate species, including birds and mammals, are also pollinators.

WHAT IS POLLINATION?

Pollination is the process of plant reproduction. Pollen from the anther must be moved to the

PARTS OF A
FLOWER

This diagram identifies some of the parts of a flower.
Pollinators move pollen from the anther of one flower
to the stigma of another. How does this diagram help you
understand how this transfer happens?

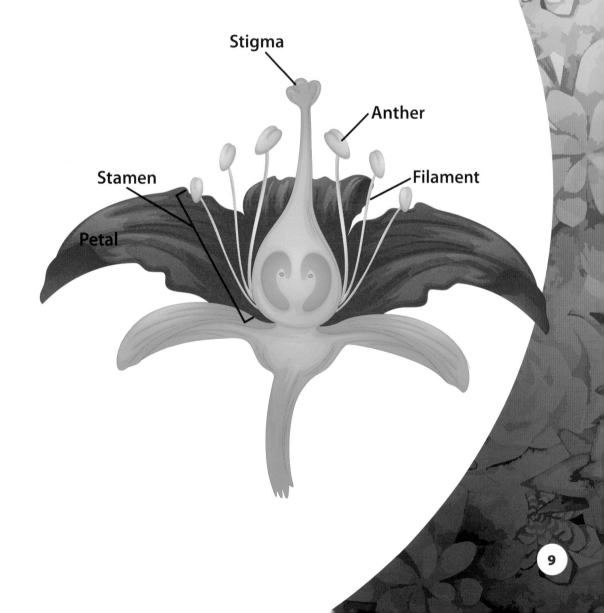

Stigma

Anther

Stamen

Filament

Petal

stigma of another flower. The stigma is the single large stem growing from the center of the blossom. This transfer allows a seed to form. That seed will grow into a new plant.

The animals that help in pollination are called pollinators. Bees are some of the most well-known pollinators. However, many other animals also pollinate. Birds, bats, ants, and beetles are other examples of pollinators. They all carry pollen from one place to another.

It is hard to see the pollination process in action. But the products of pollination are easy to find. All a person has to do is go to the grocery store. Many fruits and vegetables need pollination. Without pollinators, the world's food sources would look very different.

STRAIGHT TO THE
SOURCE

In a 2015 report, the US government explained the importance of protecting pollinators:

> *Many pollinators are in serious decline in the United States and worldwide. Preventing continued losses of our country's pollinators requires immediate national attention. . . . Some three-fourths of all native plants in the world require pollination by an animal, most often an insect, and most often a native bee. Pollinators, most often honey bees, are also responsible for one in every three bites of food we take, and increase our nation's crop values each year by more than 15 billion dollars. [Left alone], these losses of our pollinators threaten agricultural production, the maintenance of natural plant communities, and the important services provided by those ecosystems.*

> Source: "National Strategy to Promote the Health of Honey Bees and Other Pollinators." *Pollinator Health Task Force*. DoD, May 19, 2015. Web. Accessed July 19, 2019.

Back It Up

The author of this passage is using evidence to support a point. Write a paragraph describing the point the author is making. Then write down two or three pieces of evidence the author uses to make the point.

BEES, BUTTERFLIES, AND OTHER INSECTS

The world's insects are the main pollinators. Bees, butterflies, flies, and ants do the most work. Beetles also help plants reproduce.

BEES

There are 16,000 species of bees around the world. All of them play a part in the pollination process. People have relied on bees for thousands of years. They don't just need bees for pollination. Honeybees make honey and

Many people are familiar with honeybees, but fewer know about bees native to North America, such as the litigated furrow bee.

HONEYBEE HOMES

Honeybees make a lot of honey and beeswax. Beekeepers take some of it from the hive. The bees need the rest for the winter. Hives are active places where as many as 80,000 bees live during the spring and summer. With so many residents, it is important to build efficiently. Inside their hives, bees build combs out of beeswax. The combs hold wax, honey, and pollen as well as bee eggs and larvae. These combs also provide bees a place to rest at night.

beeswax. They make so much that people can take some without harming the bees. Humans domesticated honeybees to use on farms.

During the spring and summer, bees are always working. Their pollination work saves the United States a lot of money. Because of their ability to pollinate crops and other plants, studies estimate that managed honeybees alone contribute $20 billion per year assisting food production. That doesn't include any of the other pollinators that also help in food production.

A bicolored agapostemon sweat bee, native to North America, pollinates a flower.

Beekeepers care for managed bee species. But wild bee species are just as important. Wild bees pollinate 80 percent of all bee-pollinated crops. All ecosystems need a variety of species. Bees and other pollinators are no different. Each pollinator has its own specialty.

PREHISTORIC POLLINATORS

Beetles are some of nature's first pollinators. These insects began pollinating flowers 150 million years ago. That is 50 million years before bees. Beetles and bees pollinate differently. Bees carry pollen with them. Beetles eat part of the flower and leave droppings from previous flowers behind. This is called mess-and-soil pollination. Beetles still pollinate flowers today. They typically feed on flowers that attract them by scent. Magnolias and water lilies are two examples.

Bees look for flowers with a lot of nectar. Nectar gives the bees energy. Bees can see types of light that people cannot. Flower centers give off ultraviolet light. Bees can see this light. Humans cannot. Bees fly to the flower's center. That is where the nectar is. Where there is nectar, there is also pollen.

Bees are built for pollination. Different species have tongues adapted to collect nectar from different flowers. Their bodies are covered in tiny hairs. These hairs collect pollen when bees land on flowers. The pollen is a little sticky. Flowers that bees are attracted to are often just big enough for a bee to land. The bee brushes up against it, and pollen rubs off on the bee. Then when the bee goes to another flower, the pollen will rub off on that other flower.

BUTTERFLIES

There are approximately 17,500 species of butterflies in the world. Many of them rely on nectar to survive. Because of this need, butterflies often act as pollinators. They have hairs on their bodies and legs. These hairs collect pollen.

Butterflies and bees are both flying insect pollinators, but they are attracted to different types of flowers. Unlike bees, butterflies need a wide landing platform. Their wings make it impossible for them to

The Julia heliconian butterfly feeds on nectar.

fit into tube-shaped flowers. Butterflies have different

adaptations that help them find plants. For example,

butterflies can see the color red. This ability allows them

to find the right flowers. Butterflies have a long tongue to sip the nectar like bees. But their taste buds are not on their tongues. Butterflies taste with their feet.

Butterflies are active during the day. The flowers that rely on butterflies to pollinate them bloom during the day. Many flowers that rely on daytime pollinators close at night. This makes sure that no other animals will take the nectar that butterflies need. In the same way, flowers that open at night close during the day. This keeps food available for nighttime pollinators.

ANTS

Ants are lesser-known pollinators. They are not as good at pollination as bees or butterflies. In fact, ants are more likely than other insect species to take nectar from plants without pollinating.

The plants that ants pollinate usually grow low to the ground. Most ants cannot fly. They do not spread pollen as far as insects that fly. Ants must walk from flower to flower. Pollen sometimes falls off during this

journey. For these reasons, ants pollinate fewer plants than bees and butterflies.

Still, because of their size, numbers, and the plants they are attracted to, ants are important pollinators. The low-growing plants that ants pollinate do not usually attract bees and butterflies.

EXPLORE ONLINE

Chapter Two focuses on the importance of insect pollinators. One insect pollinator is the bee. Bees do a lot of work for the world's pollination needs. The website below talks about how bees pollinate. It also talks about how many plants they pollinate. After reading the article, what are some ways you could help bees?

HOW MANY FLOWERS CAN A BEE POLLINATE?
abdocorelibrary.com/pollinators

The flowers ants help pollinate are sometimes a similar color to their leaves.

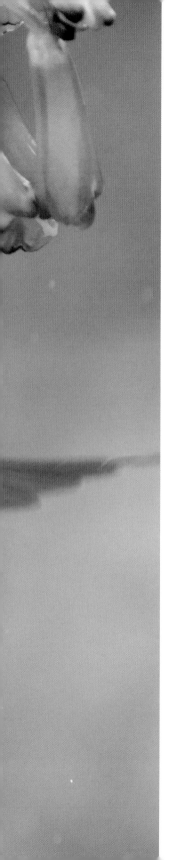

BIRDS AND BATS

I nsects aren't the only pollinators. Birds, bats, and many other animals are also important pollinators in ecosystems. Birds pollinate during the day. Bats work at night. Many people think of these animals as eating insects or seeds. However, many bird and bat species enjoy the sweet nectar of flowers.

BIRDS

Around the world, 2,000 species of birds seek out flowers for their nectar. Bird pollinators exist on every continent except Antarctica. In the United States, hummingbirds are the most common birds that feed on nectar. They pollinate wildflowers.

Hummingbirds help pollinate many flowers.

Hummingbirds are tiny. Some weigh as little as a penny. However, they eat a lot. They need a lot of energy. Their hearts beat 1,200 times per minute. A healthy human heart beats 60 to 100 times per minute. While hummingbirds migrate, they feed often. Their long, thin beak is perfect for tube-shaped flowers. At the bottom of a flower is a collection of nectar. The hummingbirds lick it with their tongues. Pollen near the top of the flower gets on the birds' head feathers. In a similar way to bees, when a hummingbird goes to the next flower, pollen brushes off.

Rain forests have other kinds of pollinating birds. One of these birds is the rainbow lorikeet.

OTHER FURRY POLLINATORS

Birds and bats are excellent pollinators. But animals that cannot fly are also pollinators. Lemurs, honey possums, and sugar gliders all help in the pollination process. These furry animals have long snouts. As they dig into flowers to get at the sweet nectar, pollen collects on their fur and paws. They carry it to the next flower.

The white-necked Jacobin hummingbird feeds on nectar in addition to insects.

It lives in Australia's tropical areas. It is also called the brush-tongued parrot. Brush-tongued parrots got their name from the shape of their tongues. They eat

A POOR SENSE OF SMELL

Flowers that attract birds usually don't have an odor. Birds have a poor sense of smell. Instead, flowers are usually brightly colored. Birds can see more colors than people can. Bright colors show birds where ripe fruits and flowers with nectar are. The one color that birds tend to avoid is white. To birds, white is a sign of danger. Many birds have white feathers that they use as a warning to others. White flowers attract different pollinators.

fruits and vegetables. However, they also enjoy nectar. Their specially shaped tongue helps them do that. The tip of their tongue has several brush-like hairs.

Unlike the hummingbird, the rainbow lorikeet can't stick its beak in many flowers. It relies instead on its tongue to collect nectar. Pollen from the flower's anthers brushes against the bird's face. Through this method, pollen is moved from flower to flower.

The rainbow lorikeet uses its tongue to eat nectar from flowers.

Mexican long-tongued bats eat agave nectar.

BATS

Many of the bats that act as pollinators live in tropical areas and deserts. They pollinate at night. The plants they pollinate also bloom at night.

Bat-pollinators mainly live in Africa, Southeast Asia, and the Pacific Islands. In North America, there are only two bats that act as pollinators. The Mexican long-tongued bat and the lesser long-nosed bat migrate to the southern United States when the cactuses bloom. The saguaro cactus and agave plant rely on bats to pollinate them when they bloom. Bats are excellent long-distance flyers. Because of this, they are able to cross-pollinate plants across large distances.

Bats pollinate many of the fruits people enjoy eating. Mangoes and bananas are just two examples of the 300 different fruits that bats help pollinate. Without bats, many of the tropical fruits people eat wouldn't exist.

FURTHER EVIDENCE

Chapter Three discusses other pollinators besides insects. What was one of the main points of this chapter? What evidence is included to support this point? Read the article at the website below. Does the information on the website support the main point of the chapter? Does it present new evidence?

POLLINATORS: HUMMINGBIRDS
abdocorelibrary.com/pollinators

HELPING POLLINATORS

Plants and pollinators work together. People rely on this relationship. Without pollinators, some popular foods would not be available. It is easy to see how important pollinators are. Still, many of them are dying. There are many threats to pollinators. Some of these include habitat loss, pesticide use, and diseases from non-native species. All of these threats are linked in some way to human actions. But people are starting to make laws to protect these important animals.

The southern border of bumblebees' range is slowly moving north because of climate change.

LOST HABITAT

One of the threats pollinators face is habitat loss. Many animals are habitat specific. That means they only live and pollinate in certain areas. These animals also need large areas of land.

Loss of habitat can stem from two main sources. One is climate change. Climate change is the warming of Earth. It is caused by greenhouse gasses. The gasses trap heat in the atmosphere. As Earth warms, animals are moving to new areas. If their usual habitat is too warm or can't sustain their food source, pollinators will stay where there is a food source. Many bees and birds are moving northward.

Another source of habitat loss is construction. When people build new houses or offices, ecosystems change. Builders cut down trees and mow flowers. These actions take away food sources. They also take away homes for the pollinators. Ground-nesting bees cannot dig in trampled soil. It is too packed down.

Clearing land for agriculture, homes, and businesses causes habitat loss.

They have to leave to find looser soil. There are some areas of land that are protected, but they are sometimes too small. The animals may not have enough space to spread out.

ARTIFICIAL POLLINATION

China grows pears and apples. However, because of pesticide use, there are not enough bees to pollinate the fruit trees in some regions. Farmers now must use artificial pollination, or hand-pollination. This means people are the ones pollinating. Some growers tried honeybees, but they did not thrive. Hand-pollination is a long process. It takes much more time for people to pollinate fruit trees than it does for bees.

PESTICIDES

Many farmers use pesticides to protect their crops. Pesticides are used to kill harmful insects that eat crops. However, these pesticides also often hurt or kill the helpful pollinators. In some areas, pollinators have left permanently.

The pollinator that is hurt the most from pesticide use is bees. A popular pesticide is neonicotinoid. Scientists have studied how it affects bees. The pesticide often kills bees. If the bee survives, the pesticide makes it difficult for the bee to reproduce. Over time, this could cause the hive to die.

PROTECTING
POLLINATORS

As of 2018, 22 US states had laws to help pollinators. There are five categories. These categories are research, pesticides, habitat protection, awareness, and beekeeping. Research laws mean people will study pollinators' health. Pesticide laws limit the use of pesticides that harm pollinators. Habitat protection laws protect existing habitats and restore other habitats for pollinators. Awareness laws create and fund programs to educate the public about pollinators. Beekeeping laws provide financial help to people who keep bees. How does this graph help you understand what states are doing to help pollinators? Do you see any patterns in which states have enacted laws?

 States with Pollinator Laws

Two studies were done on neonicotinoid in 2017. One was in Canada on honeybees. The other focused on three different bee species in the United Kingdom, Germany, and Hungary. Researchers found that it was not just the bees near farms that were dying. Hives miles away were also affected. That's because this kind of pesticide dissolves in water. When farmers water their crops or when it rains, the pesticide runs off into the waterways. The contaminated water is soaked up by flowers downstream. The chemicals stay in the flowers. They spread to the bees when they come for nectar and pollen. Bees spread it to more bees when they return to their hive.

Even more concerning is how long the pesticides are dangerous to bees. People once thought that bees were only at risk when the crops were flowering. However, the studies showed that pesticides stay in the soil and waterways throughout the whole growing season. This means that many different plants are affected.

NON-NATIVE SPECIES

Sometimes people introduce new species to control a pest. This can work for a little while. However, there can be negative consequences when a species is introduced to an ecosystem where it is not normally found. These species can bring diseases with them. They can also become predators of the native pollinators.

For example, the Asian lady beetle is not native to North America. It is an invasive species there. It eats monarch caterpillars. This means that monarch butterfly populations have been shrinking for years.

A FUTURE WITHOUT POLLINATORS?

Pollinator populations have been dropping. Scientists are worried about what a world without pollinators would look like. While small farms could hand-pollinate, that is not a sustainable method for most crops. Plants and pollinators work together to create a balanced ecosystem. Without pollinators, many of the fruits and vegetables that people enjoy would disappear. Animals who eat those fruits and vegetables would also die out.

The lady beetle, combined with habitat destruction, has had a major impact on the butterfly population.

Non-native plants can be dangerous for pollinators too. They can take over an ecosystem. They take nutrients and sunlight away from the native plants. This kills native plants that the pollinators need to survive.

Non-native plants also have diseases and fungi that can hurt insects and other animals. For example, diseases have hurt bees. Bacteria and fungi usually attack young bees. When they are still in their larval stage, bees are very vulnerable. When larvae die, there are fewer bees to take the place of older bees. If the hive does not recover from the disease, it will die.

REASON TO HOPE

Pollinators are an important part of every ecosystem. Without pollinators, the variety of food that people eat would be much smaller. Trees and bushes that rely on pollinators would slowly die. Pollinators face a lot of challenges in Earth's warming and changing landscape.

When Kedar Narayan was eight years old, he made an app that helps people identify pollinators and make pollinator gardens. The app is called Pollinator for a Pet.

But there is reason to be hopeful. There are steps that every person can take to make their homes and communities more pollinator-friendly.

Many conservation efforts are underway. Local communities are playing their part. People have started larger state-wide projects too. Part of this conservation effort is through habitat restoration. Governments often fund prairie and wetland restoration projects. Prairies and wetlands have many of the plants that pollinators need for their diet.

These habitat restoration projects aren't only good for pollinators. They also help keep ecosystems in balance. Restoring habitats to their natural appearance brings back many species of plants and animals. An ecosystem works in a cycle. All plants and animals are necessary to keep a habitat healthy.

Habitat restoration takes a lot of time. It can be expensive. But small actions can make a big impact. An easy thing many families can do is plant a bee garden. Bee gardens are collections of native plants that pollinators love. Every community has different pollinators, so different plants are needed. But bee gardens can be for more than just bees. Different types of flowers will attract birds and butterflies. Pollinators use the nectar for energy, especially as they migrate to warmer areas. A backyard garden is a great place for pollinators to rest and get a snack.

If everyone pitches in on restoring habitat and fighting climate change, pollinators will thrive. People must be willing to work with pollinators and ecosystems so that Earth stays in balance.

STRAIGHT TO THE
SOURCE

Ed Spevak is an insect expert at the Saint Louis Zoo. Spevak wrote a letter about the importance of educating people about insects:

> *Getting people into the field is but the first step in affecting conservation actions. To affect change people need to know what they are conserving. Field guides have the potential to expand the education of individuals regarding bumblebees as well as other types of bees. It has been argued that education alone is insufficient to instill change, yet is undeniable that the advent of fields guides for various taxa has inspired and encouraged people to explore the natural world . . . swelled the ranks of concerned individuals . . . and increased conservation advocacy.*

> Source: Edward Spevak. "One Zoo's Journey around the World with Native Bees." *TITAG*. TITAG, n.d. Web. Accessed August 1, 2019.

Consider Your Audience

Adapt this passage for a different audience, such as your younger friends. Write a blog post conveying this same information for the new audience. How does your post differ from the original text and why?

FAST FACTS

- Pollinators move pollen from flower to flower. This enables flowers to reproduce.

- Many plants, including many crops that people eat, rely on pollinators to reproduce.

- Bees, butterflies, ants, birds, bats, and beetles all act as pollinators.

- Bees eat nectar from flowers. In the process, they carry pollen to other flowers.

- There are 16,000 bee species worldwide.

- Wild bees are some of the most important pollinators. They pollinate 80 percent of all bee-pollinated crops.

- Butterflies typically pollinate flowers with wide landing spaces.

- Ants pollinate some plants, but they are not as effective as bees.

- Hummingbirds are well-known bird pollinators. They hover by flowers while eating the nectar.

- Some other birds, such as the rainbow lorikeet, also eat nectar and pollinate flowers.

- Some bat species, including the Mexican long-tongued bat and the lesser long-nosed bat, pollinate cactus and agave plants, among others.

- Pollinator populations are at risk because of climate change, habitat loss, pesticide use, and non-native species.

- People can work to restore pollinator habitats and plant gardens with flowers that pollinators eat to help pollinators thrive.

STOP AND THINK

Tell the Tale

Chapter One of this book talks about how a blue orchard mason bee works to pollinate apple trees. Imagine you are a beekeeper. Write 200 words about your orchard and the bees that help you. How could you make your orchard more inviting to the bees?

Why Do I Care?

Maybe you do not live in a place where there are many plants for pollinators. But that doesn't mean you can't think about ways to help the environment. How do pollinators affect your life? What do you think would be different if pollinators weren't a part of our world?

Another View

This book talks about the role pollinators play in our world. As you know, every source is different. Ask a librarian or another adult to help you find another source about pollination. Write a short essay comparing and contrasting the new source's point of view with that of this

book's author. What is the point of view of each author? How are they similar and why? How are they different and why?

You Are There

Chapter Four of this book talks about ways people can help pollinators. Imagine you are in a backyard garden specially designed for pollinators. Write a letter to your friends telling them about the garden. What animals and plants do you see? Be sure to add plenty of detail to your notes.

GLOSSARY

adaptation
a change made so
one is able to live in
an environment

domesticated
raised and managed
by people to live easily
with people

ecosystem
a community of living things
and their surroundings and
how they work together

efficient
able to do a task quickly
and well

invasive species
a species that is not native
to a certain habitat and is
harming native species there

larva
the young form of an insect
that does not have wings
and often does not look like
the adult form

migrate
to routinely travel from one
area to another

reproduce
to make offspring

restoration
the act of bringing
something back to its
original state

stigma
a pad extending straight
up from the center of the
flower that collects pollen
for fertilization

ONLINE RESOURCES

To learn more about pollinators, visit our free resource websites below.

Visit **abdocorelibrary.com** or scan this QR code for free Common Core resources for teachers and students, including vetted activities, multimedia, and booklinks, for deeper subject comprehension.

Visit **abdobooklinks.com** or scan this QR code for free additional online weblinks for further learning. These links are routinely monitored and updated to provide the most current information available.

LEARN MORE

Wassall, Erika. *Bees Matter*. Minneapolis, MN: Abdo Publishing, 2016.

Woolf, Alex. *You Wouldn't Want to Live without Bees!* New York: Scholastic, 2017.

INDEX

About the Author

Martha London is a writer and educator. She lives in the Twin Cities in Minnesota. When she isn't writing, you can find her hiking in the woods.